BLUFF YOUR WAY
IN THE
GREAT OUTDOORS

Brock and Kate Fowler

CENTENNIAL PRESS

ISBN 1-57143-002-4
U.S. edition © Copyright 1990 by Centennial Press
British edition © Copyright 1985 by the Bluffer's Guide

Printed in U.S.A.
All Rights Reserved

RDR Books P.O. Box 5212, Berkeley, CA 94705

THE GREAT OUTDOORS

When it comes to the Outdoors, there's no consensus about just what's Great and what isn't. One person's Great Outdoors is a lakeside cabin with flush toilets, hot shower, television, and fax machine, while another's is a snake-infested jungle 300 miles from the nearest rat-ridden trading post.

Few cultural gaps are wider or more difficult to bridge than the abyss between those brought up to enjoy hiking up a mountainside through a swarm of deer flies while a 50-pound pack provides a constant reminder of what Sir Isaac Newton was talking about when he said gravity was a *law* and those very different people brought up to believe that no outdoor activity ought to be undertaken if it promises to be more arduous than a poolside cocktail party. These two types might as well belong to different species or hail from different planets, so huge is the cultural divergence between them. People who hate — or think they hate — the Great Outdoors usually manage to avoid it. Life is a curious adventure, though, and the bizarre concatenation of happenstance betimes conspires to lure the most fanatically indoor-oriented among us into forays in the Great Outdoors. Often it happens in youth when the One True Love proves perfect in every respect except for an outlandish enthusiasm for camping. When the One True Love suggests a safari, the problem for the bluffer reaches the acute stage. What sort of person would disappoint the One True Love by blurting out the inconvenient truth that camping sucks? No . . . it's a classic folly of young love that some facts must be suppressed. Sometimes the image of being a good sport who just loves sloshing around in mosquito-happy swamps must be maintained at all costs. For this reason, and for variations on it, many of the people who leave the comfort of their homes to go gallivanting around the Great Outdoors are bluffing. They have no idea what they're doing so far from the Great Indoors of VCRs and microwaves. Sometimes they wish they were home, and sometimes they wish they were dead.

This book will help the bluffer endure the Great Outdoors. We even think the more open-minded bluffers may actually have some fun. We know this for sure: you multiply your chances for both survival and enjoyment if you have the right amount of gear and avoid truly dumb mistakes that thousands of people make all the time.

Five Reasons to Go Camping

(1) to eschew the angst-ridden stress of the urban rat race

(2) to commune with the awesome beauties of unspoiled wilderness

(3) to discover your essential self in the reverent serenity of nature

(4) to test your mettle under primitive conditions similar to those which shaped our ancestors

(5) to escape temporarily from
    (A) your boss

(B) your mate
(C) your creditors
(D) your responsibilities
(E) all of the above

A Word of Warning

If you know virtually nothing about camping in the Great Outdoors but you've decided to venture into the depths of the Amazon jungle or undertake a trek by dog sled above the Arctic Circle, you must do two things at once or sooner:

First, you must get a complete wilderness survival book. *Bluff Your Way in the Great Outdoors* is only a handy compendium for the tenderfoot considering a modest foray into forest or field. A young mother contemplating a week in the woods with her son's Cub Scout den should find this useful. A street-smart city guy trying to impress a yuppie girl who learned wilderness survival at a posh private school in Vermont could use this book before venturing on a canoe trip in Quebec with her and a couple of her rich, outdoorsy chums. A middle-aged businessman thinking that a week hiking in the Rocky Mountains might reduce both his stress and his cholesterol will find good stuff here. This is a primer for the abecedarian camper, a basic guidebook for the bluffer.

Second, if you know virtually nothing about camping but are determined to begin with a trek across the Gobi or a bushwhack through the highlands of New Guinea, think again. Medical students don't perform heart transplants. High school athletes don't play linebacker in the Super Bowl. Someone who has barely mastered the dog paddle doesn't attempt to swim the English Channel. The Great Outdoors is splendid, awe inspiring, adventurous, and good clean fun. You can find serenity, wisdom, beauty, even renewal in the Great Outdoors. Everything good that's been said about nature is true and vastly understates the case. Words literally fail to convey the sheer doggone wonderfulness of the natural world. The outdoor life is as hale, hearty, healthy, and hokey as it's cracked up to be by its most hyperbolic admirers. But (there's always got to be a but) the wilderness at its wildest can be *almost* as dangerous as Central Park at midnight, as inconvenient as a rush-hour LA freeway gridlock, and as complicated as the London *Times* Sunday crossword.

Wilderness survival is a complicated business. It takes some time to transform a city slicker, lounge lizard, or couch potato into Davy Crockett or Crocodile Dundee. Think of learning to camp as akin to learning to fly a plane. Both require some expert advice, good equipment, and lots of time to practice under forgiving conditions. In our misty, rose-colored cultural memories of halcyon days when Conestoga wagons bloomed on the prairies and brave and stalwart folks pushed on toward the West, we're convinced that everyone from Pappy on down to little Emmy Lou could cheerfully chop wood, build a fire, and drill a sidewinder at forty paces—all before breakfast. Now, you lament to anyone within earshot, kids from the urbs and burbs are more likely to buddy up with a Walkman than with the wilderness. But that's okay. People who love the Great Outdoors take devilish delight in introducing the tenderfoot to its strenuous pleasures.

Testing Your Character in
the Great Outdoors

Many people feel a deep need to escape from the hurly-burly of the urban rat race into the Great Outdoors in quest of their true identity. The wilderness has a way of reducing things to their essential components, with all that is artifice stripped away.

Suppose you're engaged to marry someone, but you keep postponing the stroll down the aisle because you're not quite certain you want to make a lifetime commitment. The Great Outdoors can solve this one for you as easily as Davy Crockett could skin a raccoon into a frontier gimme cap. You simply take your fiancé camping in the mountains in May during the black fly season. If your intended can maintain a cheerful demeanor under the onslaught of skatey-eight zillion voracious black flies, you have yourself a real gem there and can go ahead with wedding bells in June . . . unless, of course, the black flies reduce you to such a ranting maniac that your beloved elopes to New Jersey with an old flame from high school.

The Great Outdoors affords many tests of character. If you suspect your mate married you for your money, you can find out by taking up rock climbing — as you dangle a thousand feet above jagged rocks, your life hanging by a thread, your spouse only a flick of a finger away from freedom and wealth, you'll experience what bullfighters call a "moment of truth." Should you be of a playful disposition, you might want to hedge your bets by putting a secret codicil in your will leaving everything to the World Wildlife Fund if you die in a rock-climbing accident.

The Great Outdoors tests spirituality as well as materialism. If you turn a corner on a woodland path to find yourself between an adorable bear cub and its snarling mother who's charging toward you at top speed, you'll find out for sure whether you're an agnostic or a Hallelujah-Amen believer.

Before You Go

When you return from the Great Outdoors, you'll want to find your Great Indoors in reasonably good shape. So

- Notify the police that you'll be away.
- Stop deliveries like newspaper, mail, and pizza.
- Arrange life support for plants, pets, and wimpy, stay-at-home teenagers.
- Disconnect important electric appliances, such as your Magic Fingers massager.
- Leave a key with a friend to check the place (someone who won't empty your liquor cabinet).

Better yet, tell *several* people where you're going and when you're due back so they'll know when to begin chewing their knuckles. If you change your itinerary or your timetable, inform them about the new details. When you get back, let them know. Invite them for a surprise slide show.

Where to Find the Great Outdoors

If you think you can just meander into the wilderness any old place at any old time, you must have been noshing on loco weed. Get with it. Didn't you see *Deliverance*?

Many of our "wilderness" areas are as crowded in July as Times Square on New Year's Eve. Some campsites in the Virgin Islands must be booked a year in advance. Many public campsites require advance registration. Many require payment of fees. Many have very detailed rules about what you can and can't do—ride horses, pitch a tent, start a fire, yodel. Some unwary campers spend their vacations sweating in a line of 4×4's waiting to get a space so they can *start* camping. So you've got to at least break out the brochures and make a couple of calls to scout out the terrain before you make a commitment—or at least your Significant Other's got to—because everybody wants to "get back to nature" these days.

The Local Yokel as Resource Person

Even the fattest tomes of lore about woodcraft and wilderness survival have to be pretty general in nature because no author knows what you're like—how old, how big, how rich, how foolish—or where you're going at what time of year for how long a stay. The advice you need most is specific advice about *your* particular outdoor adventure. When you get close to your destination, when you arrive by car or plane in a hamlet or village near your chosen wilderness, go to a wharf or saloon or gas station in search of a grizzled old codger with a name like Campfire Al or Backpack Joe. If he offers you a plug of chewing tobacco, so much the better. This is the kind of guy who knows what you need to know.

Be warned, though. They may consider you a captive curiosity and tell you more than you want to know. Grizzled old coots with names like Fishbait Bill or Gumboot Bob usually gush forth with a steady stream of folksy banalities they consider a Philosophy of Life. When it comes to a Philosophy of Life, stick to the likes of Aristotle or Montaigne or Jefferson or Helen Gurley Brown or Hugh Hefner or somebody with a sophisticated appreciation of life's intricate possibilities, not some superannuated sourdough who spent most of the twentieth century in the boondocks swapping tall tales over camp coffee and backbacon. By the same token, a garrulous old coot who has trekked the locale for decades is an ideal source of advice about your gear and the best trails.

If you have neither the time nor the inclination to chew the fat with bucolic old-timers, you might try the proprietor of the local sporting goods store. Since he wants to sell you as many expensive items as possible, he may not be entirely disinterested, but at the very least, his shop will stock the gear required by local campers who know what they're doing.

Don't forget the local forest ranger, who can tell you where you may legally go or not go. Should you go into the woods in northern Maine, for example, and blunder onto the estate of some affluent sorehead, you may find yourself charged with criminal trespass, listening to a local lawman read you your Miranda rights in a Down-East accent. A night in the hoosegow will cast a pall over the most carefully planned expedition.

A local scoutmaster ought to have plenty of useful information, or a weather-beaten woman wearing a fedora festooned with fishing lures. Nothing beats getting the lay of the land from a local.

Base Camp

If you're really bluffing, really uncertain about venturing into the wilderness, consider establishing a base camp—like in "home base." If you're camping with small children, a base camp's a good idea anyway. Your base camp should be a short hike from your car, enabling you to carry in as many creature comforts as possible or make a quicker getaway if camping proves too excruciating to endure. A base camp eliminates some of the worst disasters of the blithly inexperienced, such as carrying too much too far and finding yourself with broken blisters and aching muscles in freezing rain on a muddy trail. Next to that, a base camp can look like a penthouse suite at the Waldorf.

Camping with Children

Camping with children is like not camping with children. Life with children, camping or not, puts a high premium on patience and a sense of life's perversities. Be aware that children *always* have to go just as you've zipped up your sleeping bag and closed your weary eyes. And they *always* want protection (against whatever they've just heard go bump in the night). But remember too that kids, hyperactively dismantling the tent because they're bored out of their minds by two days of rain, are a wonderful excuse to check into a motel.

Supervision of kids has to be much better in the Great Outdoors than in the pretty good indoors. For example, many kids are fascinated by and like to pet long-haired caterpillars, but 50 or more species have poisonous hairs that may cause severe allergic reactions, so you'll have to dissuade your budding zoologists. You won't, of course, know the difference between the good guys and the bad guys, larvawise, but that shouldn't bother you. Just pronounce them all poisonous, endowing each with a two-part, Latinate-sounding name like *caterpilus horridus*, and don't let anybody touch anything fuzzy.

Pets in the Great Outdoors

You may be tempted to tote your Persian or your poodle along with you to frolic in the fields and forests. But they may not thank you—they can get a snoutful of quills if they get playful with a porcupine, a peltful of stench if they try to face down a skunk, and a mouthful of teeth if they encounter a bear. Tropical fish don't present these problems, but the aquarium can be awkward to portage and may splash on bearers when steep grades must be negotiated.

How Much Should You Carry?

How much should you carry? If you're a master bluffer, the answer is, of course, nothing. Maneuver someone else into carrying everything by suggesting that you're concerned about their sedentary lifestyle and are graciously giving up your chance to play pack animal in the interest of their health. If you're a neophyte bluffer, however, you'll never get away with it, and your only recourse is simply to carry as *little* as possible. Backpacking is the ultimate proof that Hesiod and Andrea del Sarto were right to argue that less is more. No other philosophy will do.

The traditional rule of thumb goes like this: an average adult male (whatever that statistical fiction might be in real life) backpacking for a week to ten days ought to carry no more than 35 pounds. A smaller person, or someone not in top physical condition, or someone with no experience backbacking ought to draw the line closer to 25 or, at the most, 30. This is much easier said than done. The most experienced campers have the devil's own time striking that delicate balance between weight and comfort, between what they can reasonably carry and what they can reasonably do without.

Common sense and money will help. Common sense will tell you not to leave behind the first-aid kit so you can pack cans of Jell-O pudding. Money will help you buy warmth and comfort at the lightest possible weight. Generally speaking, the lighter it is the more it costs. In the final analysis, you'll face difficult choices. Do *not* choose to pack 50 pounds. One of the most experienced hikers of them all, Colin Fletcher, author of *The New Complete Walker,* felt he had to carry 66½ pounds when he began his trek through the Grand Canyon, and he declared that this "just about takes the joy out of walking." He's being facetious, of course. A 66½-pound pack takes the joy out of *living.*

Don't delude yourself into thinking that knapsack design can let you defy the laws of physics. The best designs properly fitted are superior to the poor designs simply slung on your shoulders, but nothing repeals the law of gravity or transforms a mere bluffer into Tarzan. An external, S-shaped, Heli-Arc frame with mesh backband, padded straps, extension bar, and hip-wrap can distribute the weight efficiently if properly adjusted, but you've still got to keep the total weight to a minimum.

You also have to train at least a little. Carry the loaded backpack (or a 35-pound Great Dane) around your apartment for an hour or two for several days before you venture into the Great Outdoors. It may provide a bit of amusement to anyone ringing your doorbell, but it will pay off. You need to know you won't get blisters, and you need to know your muscles are up to the challenge. If they aren't, you don't want to discover this after slogging seven hours along a muddy mountain trail.

Gravity isn't the only law of Sir Isaac Newton's you must remember. There's also this one: every action tends to have an equal and opposite reaction. If you decide you've just got to carry 50 pounds, you also better decide to camp very close to your car and to start early so you can rest often. You might also want to hire a Sherpa guide to carry the pack for you. Amazingly enough, however, there are few Sherpa guides offering their services in the boondocks of America.

A Camping Checklist

The Basics

Having warned you against packing too much weight, we must now warn you against packing too little. This checklist is an exercise in the obvious. Even so, you need this checklist or your own equivalent because you don't want to find yourself waving bye-bye to the helicopter which has deposited you three weeks from the nearest trading post without at least the basics. If you think no camper ever forgot matches, or a compass, or a flashlight, think again.

Tent – If you imagine you can do without a tent by sleeping under the stars, you're not a bluffer . . . you're what expert campers call a "ninny." If you think you can rig rustic lean-tos or find caves or handy overhanging ledges, forget it. You need a tent. You need a good tent. If there's a lot of rain and mud and cold and wind, you may be miserable even in a good tent, but without a good tent, you're going to wish you were being interviewed by the Gestapo instead of slowly freezing your digits off in the muck.

Sleeping Bag — Don't convince yourself you can make do with some sort of makeshift "bedroll" consisting of blankets and a poncho. Such a bedroll is for crashing in the game room of a sorority house, not for surviving outdoors in the black nights of teeth-chattering, goose-bumpy insomnia. You want the best sleeping bag you can afford. Unless it's summer in the South, you want a foam pad too.

Knapsack — Even the wrong knapsack is better than schlepping into the woods like a bag lady with your gear stuffed higgledy-piggledy into whatever receptacles you found in the garage or attic.

Knife — Whether you opt for a big, bad Bowie knife or a gadget-infested Swiss Army knife, be sure the thing is sharp.

Can Opener — If you carry canned food, don't forget the opener. Some Boy Scout knives have can openers. Just be sure you don't find yourself trying to gnaw the cans open with your teeth.

Rope — You need rope to secure your tent in high wind, to suspend food where it won't lure bears into your sleeping bag, and to rig a travois if someone is injured. Maybe, just maybe, you won't need rope, but if you need it, it had better be in your pack and not in the hardware store. When you need rope, nothing else will quite do.

Ax—Whether you spell it *ax* or *axe,* you need one. If you think you can get by with a hatchet, well . . . maybe so. A hatchet is better than your bare hands or your pocket knife, certainly, but it's really designed to split kindling.

Shovel—You need a shovel to dig your latrine, to bury your kitchen waste, to toss dirt on your campfire, and to dig for buried treasure when you're bored to tears cooling your heels in the boondocks with nothing better to do.

Bucket—You need to lug water from where nature puts it to where you want it. A collapsible bucket is just the thing.

Compass—Unless you're very familiar with the trail (in which case you aren't really bluffing), you need, at the absolute minimum, a general idea of what direction is in and what direction is back out. Alas, alack, and welladay, a general notion of the correct direction and a cheapie compass you don't know how to use may be worse than no help—they may convince you to go in the wrong direction.

Canteen—The kind of canteen you select reveals the kind of romantic you are. You can carry an army-surplus canteen like John Wayne had to keep the sands of Iwo Jima out of his water; you can carry a fat, western canteen with plaid sides like Mexican banditos throw away when the buzzards begin to circle overhead; you can carry a wineskin like the sheik of Araby brings when into your tent he creeps (without no pants on); or you can carry one of those flattish plastic thingies. Don't carry Kool-Aid in an aluminum canteen, and don't fill a canteen at a stream or pond, however pristine the water looks.

First-Aid Kit—Unless you're camping in midwinter snow, be sure your kit has snake-bite gear with instructions.

Personal Hygiene Items—Toothbrush, toothpaste, soap, mousse, whatever.

Flashlight—Be sure it's sturdy. Carry a spare bulb and fresh spare batteries.

Matches—*Lots* of matches in a waterproof match case in the event your rubbing-two-sticks-together technique is a little rusty.

Cooking Utensils—Whether you opt for a simple mess kit or a portable kitchen with stove, you need a pan and a dish and a cup and a fork and stuff. If you think you can live two weeks in the bush eating cold food with your fingers, you're right, but you won't like it.

Clothing—Remember to carry clothes for the worst situation you might face. If you head up mountains in spring or fall, a freak storm can plunge you into midwinter conditions. If it rains day after day, you need changes of clothing that dry quickly.

Food—Decide between canned food, dehydrated food, and ordinary fast food. Try to favor the lightweight stuff. Be sure you have enough. A backpacker needs 3,200 to 3,800 calories a day, about double your ordinary needs. Light as they are, don't be tempted to try to make do with 64 packages of Twinkies.

Camera – If you *hate* the Great Outdoors and vow never to venture beyond the pale of urban amenities again, you'll want to have photographs of yourself on this trek as proof that you *once* went adventuring in the wilderness.

This is a very basic list. The list in the appendix of the *L.L. Bean Guide to the Outdoors* contains 150 items. Of course, a cynic might suspect that the *L.L. Bean Guide* would have a long list because L.L. Bean wants to sell you the stuff, but in fact, the items on its list are useful as can be. They mention a watch, sunglasses, sunscreen, insect repellent, toilet paper, aluminum foil, trash bags, a cribbage board, jumper cables in case your car's battery runs down while you're off in the woods, extra shoelaces, even optional gaiters. Most books have longer checklists than this. Unfortunately, a much longer list and you'll need more elephants than Hannibal had just to cart the stuff.

Specialized Gear

Unless you're a very rich bluffer, avoid spending a ton of money on fancy camping gear until you learn

(1) whether you'll ever go camping again
(2) if you do, what kind of camping it will be

Borrow and scrounge gear, getting advice about it from the lenders. The reason you can get away with this is that perspicacious bluffers make sure that their outings are relatively brief forays into relatively safe wilderness in relatively pleasant weather. Bluffers should never allow themselves to be seduced into spending two weeks climbing a dangerous mountain in midwinter. That's kamikaze camping. They'll opt for summer weekends in the Catskills or in a park with rangers to warn them against their more self-destructive impulses. And as a bonus, if you can borrow gear from seasoned campers, you may wind up with better stuff than you would have bought.

Tent

Borrow a tent too—from someone who's done the sort of camping you expect to do. If fate forces you to buy a tent, do some research first—talk to campers, read consumer magazines, grill the salespeople in the sporting goods store. There's no ideal tent. Whatever tent you decide to take, pitch it at least once in your backyard; if you pitch it in your living room, don't forget you need an adequate supply of pegs. You don't want to learn that you're missing several key elements during a freezing rainstorm in the back of beyond.

If you have one of the new nylon tents with a funny little hat, be sure to put the hat on and to snug its guys so that it pulls away from the main tent. The tent is not waterproof, and the water that runs off the little hat will soak through your tent unless you pull it out far enough with the little ropes. Also, remember, a waterproof bottom not only keeps moisture out—it also keeps moisture in.

Older Boy Scout manuals will tell you to dig a trench around your tent to keep water away. But point out condescendingly to anyone in your party insensitive enough to try it that the conservation ethic frowns on this. In fact, the conservation ethic scowls menacingly at this. Those ruts require years to heal, it they heal at all. Sometimes runoff turns them into permanent gashes. With millions of campers pitching tents on more millions of sites, the cumulative damage is dreadful to contemplate.

Try to borrow a tent with adequate ventilation. Those little pup tents are okay for one nine-year-old in a backyard, but two adults could create a swamp in one on a summer night. Be sure the tent has adequate netting—not torn to shreds, not with holes so big that no-see-ums breeze right through.

If you're backpacking, you need a lighter-weight tent than if you're going by canoe or pitching a base camp near your car. If you'll be camping with kids, you need a *big* tent so they, and you, don't go berserk on rainy days. If you intend to sleep above the tree line, you need a mountain tent with little wind resistance and lines that break before fabric tears.

Sleeping Bag

Sleeping bags come in three basic shapes: rectangular, barrel, and mummy. The rectangular bag has room to roll over, but that room results in heat loss. If you want comfort, buy the rectangle; if you want image, buy the mummy. The rectangle is what you need if you hope to persuade another camper to snuggle with you against the nighttime cold—rectangular bags zip together nicely. When you buy a bag, get in it and try the zipper from the inside at least twice. If the zipper catches even a little, try another bag. Remember that down is good insulation because of the little spaces between the little feathers; as soon as you lie on the down, no more little spaces and no more insulation:

with a down-filled sleeping bag, you *must* have a soft foam mattress.

Canoe

The classic advice about canoes was embodied in the immortal remark of French-Canadian explorer Louis Joliet to missionary Père Jacques Marquette when the latter advised Joliet to use a different stroke as they negotiated the Sault Sainte Marie—Joliet said, *"Pas de le Rhône que nous."* (It was this pithy wisdom which prompted the citizens of Illinois to name a city after him, proof that you can paddle your way to immortality in a birch-bark canoe.)

As a bluffer, you don't need to panic at the prospect of paddling your own canoe, but paddle around a calm pond on a nice day to get the hang of the thing.

There are wooden canoes, aluminum canoes, and fiberglass canoes. There are even kits so you can build your own canoe. The one you want is . . . ah! That depends. Wooden canoes are beautiful but expensive, and they need a lot of upkeep. Fiberglass canoes are okay, though some are too narrow or shallow. The virtues of the aluminum canoe are many, making it by far the most popular in the United States—it's tough and largely maintenance free; but (there's *always* got to be a but) its extreme buoyancy can make it hard to handle in the wind. One good rule is to prefer a large canoe: overloading is a real danger, and a larger craft offers you better handling when loaded.

The standard rule is that your paddle should reach from the floor to your chin, though most experts prefer them even longer—floor to eyes, or even a bit taller than you are. A wider blade gives better control but is more tiring to use. If you have two different paddles, use the wider blade in the stern (that's the *rear* to landlubbers, so always say *stern.*). Any paddle should have a thin edge, and no paddle should be used to pole a canoe. Be sure to have an extra paddle—it's as easy to break or lose a paddle as it is to drop toast butter side down—or at least a pudding stick, a short, two-foot emergency paddle. Remember, a paddle that's too short will make you hunch over, increasing your work and your backaches and ruining your image. Go ahead and sit on the seat in calm water. In choppy water, kneel down for better stability. About this choppy water . . . avoid it.

You already know about different strokes for different folks. There are dozens of canoe strokes, each with dozens of names. You can take a canoe course, read a book, or muddle through by trial-and-error. Put the more experienced paddler in the stern, where the paddle can be used as a rudder. Be sure, of course, to announce to your group that the experienced paddler, such as you are, always sits in the bow. If you have two inexperienced people in the canoe, be sure your trial-and-error is done in Lake Smooth Sailing.

Make certain your canoe has a painter—a rope 20 feet long tied to the bow. *Always* secure the canoe at night; sometimes a canoe responds to wind like a kite, sailing into the air and away.

The most dangerous thing most people do with a canoe is lash it to the top of a car with a single strand of clothesline. At freeway speeds, the force of the wind against the canoe can reach hurricane force and turn you into a reluctant UFO. Use strong lines, two of them, rigged to pull diagonally to both sides, front and rear.

Your canoe should be equipped with life preservers, and you should have them on. That's probably why all the experts agree that it's sometimes all right to stand up in a canoe. What's all right for an expert, however, may be sheer folly for a bluffer. If you must do something risky in a canoe, forget standing up – make love instead. You're less likely to capsize and more likely to have fun. If you make love standing up in a canoe, be sure to have someone take pictures – without them, the editors of the *Guinness Book of Records* will never believe it.

Catalytic Heaters

No matter what it says on the box or in the directions, *never* use any catalytic heater in a tent or cabin without scads of ventilation. For that matter, anytime you burn any sort of fuel – kerosene, wood, propane – in an enclosed space, be certain to provide adequate ventilation.

Lanterns

The network hood that acts as a filament to give off brilliant light when incandescent is called a mantle. Some mantles contain beryllium and give off very toxic beryllium oxide fumes, a potential cause of beryllium disease. To be on the safe side, never preburn a mantle indoors, and lean away from the lantern when lighting it to avoid inhaling the fumes.

Binoculars

We don't know much about binoculars, but we do

know our old binocs have given us a lot of pleasure when we remembered them, and we were also sorry to find ourselves on a mountaintop or scenic vista without them. One consumer testing service says that there's little difference between expensive and inexpensive models as far as purely ocular matters are concerned, but they recommend Japanese binoculars for their quality control. It seem there's been something since 1959 called the Japanese Telescopes Inspection Institute, and the JTII seal of approval is a good thing to look for.

Hatchet

It's been said that the "telling blow against the hatchet is that no professional woodsman – guide, trapper, timber cruiser, logger, or woods surveyor – carries one. Only the Romanticist – inept and bungling at the woodpile – hangs one on his belt and walks like a side-hill gopher." Bluffers should never consider carrying a hatchet – no matter how cute it is. What you need is an ax.

Ax

Maybe the most important thing about an ax for bluffers is leather boots. After that, a long handle. How long depends, but prefer the longer-handled poleax to the shorter-handled Hudson's Bay. To see why, swing an invisible ax and miss what you're chopping by falling short – the long handle drives the head into the ground but the short handle can finish the arc at your foot, ankle, or shin. Having said all this, it's also necessary to say that the conservation ethic opposes your chopping anything that nature hasn't already knocked down. Living trees and standing dead timber alike ought to be let alone. (Many kinds of birds depend upon standing dead trees or snags for their homes.) Remember that the ideal is to leave the wilderness as if you'd never been there, which, of course, you may wish were true.

First-Aid Kit

Don't go into the woods, even on a short afternoon hike, without a first-aid kit. Don't scrimp on first-aid items because of weight or expense—the rule remains "Better safe than sorry." Pack the items in an actual kit so they're together, easy to find. Wrap the kit in a waterproof bag and mark it clearly in big letters so that even the terminally myopic can find it in a hurry—the person who knows what it looks like may be the one injured. In addition to the basics, be sure to include necessary medications for every person in the party.

New Products

As the prospectors were wont to say, "There's gold in them thar hills!" The big money to be made in camping equipment lures entrepreneurs of ingenuity to introduce hundreds of new products every season. A backpack called the Osprey Silhouette is supposed to carry 5,000 cubic inches of gear with advanced design and a price tag of over $250. Something called the Ecotat Systems Freedom Shelter can be slung like a fanny pack, weighs less than five pounds, and claims to be poncho, tent, and hammock, for about $200. The Bibler I-tent weighs three and a half pounds, claims to be the only single-walled waterproof/breathable tent made in America, and costs nearly $400. The Edko

Piccolo daypack has a cult following for its handy pockets and flashy designs. The ZZip Ztove is a cute little one-pound woodstove (with a cute little name) with its own devoted aficionados, but a gizmo cunningly called the Bakepacker has its fans too. A Solar Lantern is very enlightened but weighs over nine pounds and costs nearly $400. Boots called Skywalks from a company called Vasque weigh less than three pounds and seem to combine some qualities of sturdy hiking boots with the lightness of sneakers; cost about $120. At $125, the Higher Altitude Pack weighs only 18 ounces but is so thin the manufacturer warns it will last only one expedition—how's that for planned obsolescence? Shop around—new products with various clever features hit the stores all the time—and what the heck, it's only money.

SKILLS

Selecting a Campsite

The classic dumb mistake is to plan too long a hike, then push on until darkness is falling before finding a campsite. Make sure there's plenty of daylight left when you choose a place to pitch camp. Select the most beautiful site and keep it pristine. While you want a sheltered spot, avoid the base of a cliff, or falling rocks may get you. Avoid dry washes or riverbeds because flash floods sweep away the unwary season after season. A waterfall is romantic, but its mist will drench everything—even lust—by midnight. A tent near the shoreline can be soaked if a brisk breeze comes up. Look around for dead trees likely to crash on your tent.

Latrines

The latrine should be on high ground so that waters seeping through will be filtered before they get to a stream or pond. Dig a slit trench 8 to 14 inches— shallower and animals may dig it up; deeper and bacterial action may not take place. Unless there's severe fire danger, set a match to toilet tissue. Leave a shovel nearby and sprinkle some dirt into the hole after each use. When you break camp, fill in the latrine and replace rocks, leaf litter, and other natural features.

The Campfire

Campfire lore takes much of a lifetime to master. As a bluffer, all you need to remember is that the theory of the fire is simplicity itself: tinder, kindling, and firewood. If you direct your group with the following and use a benevolent but authoritative tone, they'll enthusiastically hop to it and get your fire burning merrily.

Be sure you site the fire on ground that's not itself a slow-burning fuel that will burn underground for a few days and then burst forth as a forest fire; the same goes for roots. Clear debris away and pile stones around any large fire—don't get the stones from a stream or lake because they may explode when inner pockets of water suddenly expand into steam. If it's windy, rig a tarp to keep the sparks from flying and the fire from raging out of control. Birch bark makes great tinder, but unless you take only curls of fluff, you can kill a living tree, so get the bark from fallen trees. Whittled shavings from a stick of softwood will do nicely. Kindling has to be *thin,* less than an inch, and placed loosely enough so that it doesn't crush the tinder as it burns. Wait until the kindling burns briskly before adding three or four sticks of firewood, stacked so air can circulate under them to create an updraft.

A *small* cookfire is best—if you can get near enough to work on the food, you're less apt to scorch things like your last packet of instant borscht or your eyebrows, and the fire's more apt to stay where it's welcome. When starting the fire, put your match on the windward side so the wind fans the new fire; inexperienced campers use the tinder as a windbreak by lighting on the lee side only to have the wind blow the flame away from the fuel you hope to ignite. Hardwood burns longer, but no campfire will last the night: have an adequate supply of firewood near at hand to add when the cold (or a raccoon) wakes you. When you're done with the fire, drown it, being sure to drench the undersides of smouldering wood.

Stories Around the Campfire

The essential thing to have around the campfire is . . . ghost stories. By long and unhallowed tradition, the time is whiled away with hair-raising tales of supernatural terror. Surrounded by miles and miles of night-blackened wilderness punctuated by strange, unnerving noises, the camper is highly susceptible to spine-tingling sensations. Before you venture into the woods, prepare yourself with some classic ghost stories. Read them on sunny days at the beach, and perhaps they'll seem less terrifying in the forest at midnight. When it's your turn to tell a tale of terror, be sure to include a blood-curdling shriek at the penultimate plot twist. If you want to see what your companions look like with snow-white hair, tell them your own version of "The Monkey's Paw" by W. W. Jacobs. Poe's "The Black Cat" is apt, albeit overfamiliar. You might have better luck by abridging F. Marion Crawford's "The Screaming Skull" or if you feel you have literary and dramatic flair, H. P. Lovecraft's "The Dunwich Horror," but don't be dismayed if your kids would rather hear "Freddie Krueger Stalks the Teenage Mutant Ninja Turtles." As the Scouts say, "Be prepared." Around a campfire, ghost stories are as essential as mosquito repellent.

Songs Around the Campfire

Individuals whose musical ability is so wretched that they dare not sing in the shower are frequently emboldened to burst into song when sitting near a wilderness campfire. Many ornithologists believe that several species of birds have gone extinct because they just lost heart when they heard one too many campers rendering "One Hundred Bottles of Beer on the Wall" or "On Top of Old Smoky." If you go camping in a group, expect to find yourself dragooned into a rustic hootenanny. Unless you're very fortunate, you'll suddenly discover that your companions have actually brought impossible-to-tune banjos, foot-long harmonicas, and kazoos that look like little slide trombones. To protect your sanity, you may want to bring earplugs or a Walkman with your favorite heavy metal tapes—Mötley Crüe begins to sound like the Mormon Tabernacle Choir in comparison to a dozen boozy campers bellowing "Home on the Range." To prove you're really a good sport, go along with the ritual incantation of the Mishmosh Indians: Owah tagu siam!

Foraging

There are lavishly illustrated books to tell you which plants are edible and which are deadly poisonous. Even in the full-color photographs, the edible plants and the deadly plants look pretty similar. In the wild, only your botonist knows for sure. Stick to freeze-dried delicacies. The canny bluffer knows that the best foraging is in the local supermarket—but food additives being what they are, foraging is dangerous even there.

Point out that wild onions are virtually indistinguishable from death camas; wild carrots are very similar to poisonous hemlock; milkweed is at certain seasons very like poisonous dogbane. Since you can't call the Poison Control Hotline from the shores of Gitche Gumee, you'd better eat food that's been certified as food. In other words, leave the grazing to the Euell Gibbons types.

Cooking

Wilderness cooking is much more a matter of philosophy than of technique. "To be or not to be" is not the question; the question is, "How much trouble am I willing to go to so I can eat like I do at home?" Some campers answer, "A great deal of trouble," while others answer, "None at all" and eat as efficiently as possible even if they don't much like the grub.

Beware of thinking your group can cook and eat as a group. Families have begun savage feuds and marriages have ended in bitter divorce because of this fallacy, and mere acquaintances will almost certainly come to blows over breakfast by Day Five. Bring stuff you're willing to prepare and eat, and then be content with it. Let the others do likewise.

Remember that you can't wash dishes in streams or ponds and that you must bury all your kitchen waste far from your camp. The more elaborate your wilderness feast, the bigger the pain in the ass. Some people actually enjoy the inconvenience, as a proof of woodcraft skills and strength of character, while others assume there's nothing better to do in the back of beyond anyway, but you might hate it. Successful bluffers obey the rule "Keep it simple" while at the same time, of course, making sure that what they do appears to be terribly complex, arcane, and woodsy. Actually, you can mix granola with powdered milk at home and just surreptitiously add water on the trail. Lots of people carry those instant breakfast drinks. Most of the stuff you need is right in the supermarket—instant mashed potatoes, rice, macaroni, spaghetti . . . all light to carry, easy to cook.

If you don't go too far into the woods for too long, you can carry a few canned goods, but then you, or someone, has to carry the cans out; that means washing them, crushing them without cutting yourself, wrapping them in something, and schlepping them back. That's a lot of fuss for a few bites of Beanie Wienies.

The freeze-dried food you buy where you get your camping gear usually tastes okay and is as convenient as room service. *But* it's a very expensive way to eat, and the packagers usually lie about the portions. A package that claims to feed four will sometimes barely satisfy one hungry camper. This varies from company to company and from item to item, but to be on the safe side, you need plenty of freeze-dried foods, probably quite a bit more than their packages suggest.

Some people take camping as an excuse to indulge in their favorite candy bars. After all, a sugar surge is quick energy and a hiker needs *lots* of extra calories. If you try this, you may learn the truth about there being too much of a good thing. Trying to get by on sugar is as bad or worse an idea in the forest than it is in the factory or on the farm. A couple of candy bars may be good for your soul's repose—that's between you and your conscience—but for the most part, stick to gorp.

Few culinary skills are more arcane than roasting a marshmallow over a campfire. Rumor runs that Julia Child and James Beard nearly came to blows during a disagreement about this subject, with Julia shouting, *"Bien cuit! Bien cuit!"* She subscribed to the *cordon noir* school, which insists that the marshmallow must be held directly in the flames until the outside is as black as a hockey puck, while he felt that the marshmallow ought to be held far from the flames until it turns from white to beige. The controversy hardly ends there. Those who want the marshmallow engulfed in flames feel it should be ingested by holding the stick above the mouth in the attitude of a sword swallower, with the melted goop dripping directly into the open mouth. Those of the opposite persuasion believe that the barely warm confection ought to be delicately removed from the stick with the fingers and eaten in several dainty bites like a small apple. As with the question of whether the planet is being visited by Unidentified Flying Objects, there's no way to compromise the opposing views. No matter how you cook and eat your marshmallow, you'll infuriate some other camper. Some people take extreme measures to avoid this situation by actually venturing into the woods *without* marshmallows! This desperate and rash act deprives the camper of an ideal outdoor food, chock full of proteins and vitamins and minerals. Some scholars insist it was the generous ration of marshmallows which enabled Amundsen to beat Scott in the race to the South Pole in 1912.

As a rule, despite the thousands of recipes for "camp

coffee," most campers prefer tea to coffee in the woods because of the awesome simplicity of the tea bag. Instant hot chocolate and bouillon are popular for the same reason. Campers using water purification tablets often like to mask the aftertaste with lemonade or iced tea.

"Camp coffee?" We thought you'd never ask! One heaping tablespoon of regular coffee for each 12 ounces of water, plus one extra for the pot. Bring the water to a rolling boil, add the coffee, cover the pot, and cook for five minutes. Remove from the fire. Now . . . to settle the grounds. This is where hearsay sets in. Some advise a half cup of cold water, others a raw egg or eggshells, still others salt. (We suggest the cold water.) Try this at home until you can produce something palatable. If you can whip up good camp coffee, nobody will notice that you're bluffing your way with freeze-dried delicacies and candy bars.

Orienteering

Some chapters on orienteering are longer than this entire book and more technical than textbooks for engineers in graduate school. There are five different kinds of compass, and to use one properly, so the experts say, you need to know about azimuth scales, declination (the difference between true north and magnetic north in your particular part of the pucker-brush), triangulation, oscillation, TOES (the mnemonic near-acronym for "to obtain eastern variation: subtract"), damping, and lots of other stuff. Don't think that a cheapie 98¢ compass and a map drawn freehand by a chum who once upon a time camped where you want to go will suffice. But as a sensible bluffer, you don't have to worry about any of this; what you do is stick to well-marked trails in good weather. Brandishing a high-tech compass and a map filled with esoteric, indecipherable topological squiggles *will* enhance your reputation, but don't start believing your own stuff and overconfidently use them to march miles in the wrong direction, far from where people will be looking for you. If you do get lost, here are a few useful tips.

First and foremost, don't panic. Sit down and reflect. Make a plan. Often, your best bet is to stay close to where you are when you realize you're lost because people will be looking for you within a reasonable distance of where you were last seen. If you decide rescue isn't coming and you must find your way out, begin with a large circle around your base camp, looking for a trail. If that fails, pick a direction and stick to it. If you have no compass, pick first one landmark and then another on the same heading.

If you start a signal fire, adding green growth will give you thicker smoke, but add it slowly or you'll simply extinguish your fire. Try to keep to open ground so you can wave a shirt or something at search planes. If you're lost in cold weather, don't try to stay awake — it's a dangerous old wives' tale that sleep will kill you; wasting heat resources pacing around pinching yourself is much more likely to finish you off.

Forget that old chestnut about following a stream down to civilization. Yes, all streams flow to the sea . . . but some disappear into swamps or huge lakes difficult to circle. If you get lost coming down a mountain, go back to the top and look for the trail. Above all, stay dry and stay calm and confident. Remember what a

great yarn this will make when you're back to civilization, determined never again to venture beyond shouting distance of the nearest delicatessen.

The Instant Field Guide

Wildflowers

You can allow your companions to lord it over you
because they know the names of wildflowers and you
don't, or you can study botany at the university for
several years. A third option is to become an instant
field guide. All you need is a bit of aplomb and a poker
face. Simply glance at a wildflower or weed, and then
invent a name for it. If anyone challenges you, calmly
maintain that the name you invented has been traditional for generations in your grandmother's neck of
the woods where you summered as a child. Here are
some ersatz names you may apply willy-nilly to
wildflowers:

- Joskin's knickers
- Wartkin
- Snoblolly
- Flatulencia
- Shepard's bloat

Birds

You don't have to invent names for birds. The real
names are funnier. Some birds aren't content with one
silly name and actually have two—the cowbird is also
called the cuckold, and the woodcock is also called the
bogsucker. When a fine-feathered friend flashes by,
insist it's one of these:

- California bushtit
- Xanthus's becard
- Beardless flycatcher
- Gutter snipe
- Dickcissel
- Alewife
- Long-winded goatsucker
- Painted lazuli

PESTS

The animals know that pests are you and your fellow campers, pestering them in their natural homes, and you can sound authentically eco-aware by saying so. However, you can simultaneously watch out for

Mosquitoes

A single mosquito in a tent can drive a saint into paroxysms of rage. By the tenth time its buzz roars in your ear like a chain saw, you may fracture your skull by bashing yourself with a savage haymaker—but the mosquito will be long gone, laughing at you from the far end of the tent. It's important to know that swatting at mosquitoes is futile. The male emits the higher buzzing sound, the one you're most likely to hear, but the male doesn't bite. So you need to swat at the female when you *don't* hear the buzzing sound. See, we told you it was futile. Although the mosquito excels at single combat, it usually attacks in swarms. The mosquito ravaged the armies of Caesar and Napoleon, so what chance do you have against it? Improve your odds by avoiding its favorite seasons and haunts. In general, mosquitoes are worse in spring than in late summer and worse in dense lowlands than in breezy open spaces. We've been assured that they like the color blue and dislike the color red, but our efforts to prove this have failed because the swarms were so huge that the people wearing red bandanas were routed quite as thoroughly as those wearing blue. Some insect repellents are effective, but they can irritate sensitive skin and must be reapplied frequently. Long sleeves and mosquito netting work well unless it's so hot and muggy that mosquitoes begin to seem the lesser evil. B-vitamins are said to repel mosquitoes and gnats by making your body odor offensive to them. Once-bitten, the twice-shy may find relief from itching with these suggested remedies: pennyroyal, vinegar, the juice of squeezed comfrey leaves, and (in the words of Ripley, you can believe it or not) meat tenderizer—the papaya extract being the secret ingredient. One last tip: many products attract biting insects, even through a fog of repellent—these include deodorants, sun-tan lotions of various sorts, hairsprays, shaving lotions, perfumes; in your attempt to smell good, you may be just asking noxious bugs from miles around to join your party.

Of course, if everyone else in your group wants to spend another week slogging through the puckerbrush and you're fed up with rusticity, you may want to splash on the cologne to attract as many mosquitoes as possible—with enough of those guys buzzing around, the most intrepid nature freak soon begins to yearn for the Greater Indoors.

Gnats to You

Prepare yourself for a shock: mosquitoes are not the most annoying insects that fly around in swarms and bite people. In spring and early summer, the black fly (or buffalo gnat) is far worse, and worse still are the smaller-yet gnats, midges, sand fleas, punkies, no-see-ums, or whatever you call them in your neck of the woods. Ordinary screening is useless against these infiltrators. When the black flies and no-see-ums swarm, indoors is the only place to be. If you decide to defy the wrath of the gnat, try rubbing a layer of baby oil on exposed skin; it's supposed to form a barrier against gnat bites. And bring along a bottle of calamine lotion to relieve the "afterbite" itching.

Gnats are sometimes confused with nits by philologists and entomologists alike (and philologists and entomologists *are* alike). Noah Webster wanted to make things consistent by spelling gnat *nat* or nit *gnit*, though it's not obvious after all this time how that would have helped.

Ticks

The tick is a nasty little parasite that imbeds its barbed proboscis under your skin and sucks your blood until it's engorged. A tick is worse than Dracula because not even Bram Stoker accused the Transylvanian count of spreading encephalitis, relapsing fever, tularemia, Rocky Mountain spotted fever, and Lyme disease. If you panic and pull one out of your skin, you may leave the head stuck in your flesh, where it can cause disease and disgust. Some suggest applying heat—a matchhead, say—and others have had success with tweezers. Mineral oil, salad oil, or butter will supposedly close its breathing pores, forcing it to back out, a maneuver the faint-of-heart might want to avoid watching. When rid of the pest, wash the wound with soap and water. Check yourself so ticks don't engorge themselves on you in secret. If you're hiking with someone with whom you'd like to become more familiar, you can check *each other* for ticks. "So much more thorough," you say. An insect repellent containing Deet (diethyltoluamide) is said to be effective against ticks, but there's some disagreement about its use—one container says to splash it on skin, but a TV expert said it's too harsh for skin and should be splashed on clothing, though the container warns against using it on synthetic fabrics or plastics. Ticks like old logs and abandoned shacks, so avoid them. Obnoxious as they are, ticks cannot be blamed for Lime disease, which is spread by tumblers of rum.

Snakes

Snake expert Norman Roberts has never been bitten, even though he hunted rattlesnakes as a boy. He says, "Ordinarily, herpetologists don't get bit because they're always looking down. Ornithologists get bit because they're always looking up." Ninety percent of snake bites occur because an unwary camper stepped on or near a snake, or reached near one to pick up something.

Many books go on at great length about which snake is which, but as a bluffer, your best bet is to be very careful where you put your hands and feet. Even Indiana Jones is afraid of snakes. Afraid of them or not, give them a wide berth.

Other Problem Critters

The Black Widow Spider—She's the one with the red

dot, whose bite stings like the jab of a needle, leaving two tiny red marks. While the bite's seldom fatal, it should be looked at by a doctor. Black widows like damp, dark places and are often found in outhouses or woodpiles. It's safer to use a grassy clearing than it is an abandoned privy.

Porcupine –The porcupine has a few thousand quills, give or take a few. They can't be shot through the air, nor are they poisonous, but they're nasty enough because short barbs work the quill deeper into your flesh and the wound may fester. Cut a quill before you try to remove it. Porcupines love salt, oil, and fat, so they'll gnaw boots or saddles or anything else with a properly sweaty taste.

Skunks – Mark Twain said the polecat makes an excellent pet because it's fond of children and is an excellent rat catcher. If one comes into your camp or into your tent, try to keep it calm. Try to keep yourself calm. If it sticks its fluffy tail in the air, that means it's becoming *less* calm. If it stamps its little forefeet, that means it's becoming downright indignant. The next step is disaster – drops of a malodorous secretion are flung ten feet in a mist that can hang in the air for hours and with a stench that can be detected for half a mile. Clothes doused by a skunk might as well be buried, though folk remedies do exist: the smoke of scalded corn meal, for example, or its modern equivalent – several dry cleanings. If your dog tangles with a skunk, wash him – the dog, not the skunk – in tomato juice and then rub dry corn meal or oatmeal into his fur to absorb the droplets of skunk oil.

Bears – "As a rule, bears won't bother you," you say to your party sagely. A mother bear, however, will *kill* you if she thinks you're menacing her cub, so if you see an adorable baby bear, don't fumble around for your camera while inching toward it for a better picture – a discreet retreat is in order. Don't keep food, especially with a scent, in your tent. Suspend food from trees some distance from your camp, ten feet up and five from the nearest tree trunk. The bear is faster than you, and the wilderness is the bear's home, not yours, so show the bear some respect.

Yeti – The Yeti is a hirsute anthropoid with hyperbolic pedal extremities. Certain tribes called this furtive carnivore the Sasquatch (he's addressed as Big-Foot and Abominable Snowman, as well). Nomenclature isn't the only confusion surrounding the Yeti. There's some dispute about whether the individuals who've reported encountering the creature were either (A) sober or (B) sane at the time of the sighting, or since. Bluffers may want to hedge their bets just to be on the safe side. The best way to lure a Yeti into camera range is to make tracks with huge boots from a swamp to your tent during spring mating season, provided that you're willing to cope with an amorous Yeti (of either sex) if one does show up. Campers wishing to make certain they *never* encounter a Yeti should avoid (A) British Columbia and (B) Amityville.

Other Things That Might Bite – Alas, there are more biting pests than we have room to name. The cone-nosed bug is called the kissing bug because it tends to bite around the mouth; the giant waterbug is also called the toebiter for obvious reasons. After a bee sting, scrape away the stinger and apply a poultice of baking soda. You may also encounter wasps, hornets, chiggers, fleas, or centipedes. Deer flies are so maddening that they cause horses (and perhaps bluffers) to bolt and run amok. There are scorpions, too, but except in the southwest, their sting is said to be no worse than that of the bee.

PERILS

Giardia

When a high concentration of campers is combined with bad backwoods sanitation, the result is often Beaver Fever, the traditional name for the condition doctors call giardiasis. It's no fun. Because the symptoms may not appear for four weeks, giardiasis may spare your vacation only to ruin your life at home or on the job. Giardiasis is caused by nasty little parasites called *Giardia lamblia.* They're spread when fresh water is polluted by animal or human waste. Because beavers move from waterway to waterway, they've been blamed for the spread of the parasite, thus the name Beaver Fever, but the sharp increase of giardiasis in recent years is because of human waste, and it would better be called Slob Fever.

You need to avoid getting it, spreading it, and ignoring it if you do get it. To avoid getting it, don't drink water from streams or lakes—no matter how clean they look, no matter how thirsty you are, no matter how natural or romantic it seems. You must boil water for ten minutes or treat it with chemicals, which may require 30 minutes, or run it through commercial filters—the alternative is to carry water from home, and for that, you need Gunga Din. To avoid spreading giardiasis, you might want to carry a chemical toilet to your base camp even if it doesn't promote your rugged image.

Poison Ivy

Poison ivy is a curse on campers and on writers alike. It's virtually impossible to warn you against the noxious growth because it's the Lon Chaney of the botanical world, the Plant-of-a-Thousand-Faces. It has, as everyone knows, three shiny leaves to a cluster. These are dark green in summer, scarlet or orange in the fall. In the spring, the plant has small white flowers which become green berries until the fall, when they turn white—prompting the folk saying "Berries white, poisonous sight." Poison ivy can appear to be a climbing vine or a low shrub. No two drawings of it look alike. No two photographs of it look alike. Not only the leaves but also the roots and stems are dangerous.

You can be infected by touching poison ivy, which secretes a poisonous oil. You can be infected by the smoke of burning poison ivy. If your dog gets into poison ivy, you can get it by petting or washing the dog. The infernal stuff stays dangerous on clothing for a year, even after laundering. Symptoms sometimes appear within a few hours after infection but sometimes not for a few days. Some cases result in mildly annoying redness with itching, but many create ugly areas of oozing blisters and some require hospitalization. Don't take poison ivy lightly.

The first thing to do is wash the infected area with . . . with what? Opinions differ. The scientist on *Newton's Apple* said soap and water to remove the poison oil, but Rodale's book of useful lore says just water because soap removes the skin's natural oil. Rubbing alchohol may help, or a paste of vitamin C, or the juice from the leaves of wild plantain, fresh catnip, or jewelweed, but of course, without your friendly botanist along, you won't be able to identify these and are very likely to rub yourself with more poison ivy. The old-faithful remedy remains calamine lotion. Pack a bottle—just in case.

Alas, there are dozens of other poisonous plants in the United States and Canada. Poison oak is most common in the southeastern U.S.A. and the west coast, while poison sumac is found in swampy areas from Florida to Maine and out to Minnesota. Try not to make their acquaintance.

Burns and Blisters

Campfires and camp stoves are out to get you and can cause terrible burns, particularly because many of the pots and procedures are unfamiliar and not your friends. It's easy to knock over a pan of boiling water when a mosquito bites you as you trip over a root in the dark. You simply *must* have a first-aid kit with sterile gauze dressings. Vitamin E squeezed from a capsule is good, and so is the juice of aloe vera plants (though you're hardly apt to be carrying them around the woods).

An ounce of prevention is worth a ton of cure when it comes to blisters. Break in new footwear gradually, long before your hiking begins. If a blister breaks, don't treat it with alcohol or merthiolate—these skin disinfectants can harm tissue. Stick to soap and water.

R&R

If you stagger out of the forest with aching muscles, mosquito-bitten flesh, sore feet from slogging through mud, bleary eyes from lack of sleep, a hollow rumbling stomach for want of palatable food, and a heavy heart from having been kept so far from your beloved soaps (both cosmetic and televisual), you need recuperation and rehabilitation in a luxury hotel with room service and Jacuzzi at your fingertips. Keep the Hilton Hotline number handy.

SEX IN THE GREAT OUTDOORS

Mother Nature is a better sex therapist than Dr. Ruth and Dr. Kinsey put together (and it's only a scandalous rumor that they ever were put together). Most sexologists believe that sex had its origins in the Great Outdoors; they deduce this hypothesis from the curious circumstance that for most of its history, the planet Earth had virtually no indoors worthy of the name. It was in field and forest that the rutting elk and the rampant stag gave sex its images of wild exuberance. Many modern city-dwellers find that the pressures of urban life make sex difficult — instead of feeling frisky, she has a migraine; instead of feeling randy, he suffers from stress-induced detumescence (don't bother to look it up; it means what you think it means). The wilderness experience can often restore such victims of modern malaise to full vigor and virility. In the words of that Casanova of nineteenth-century New England, Henry David Thoreau, "We need the tonic of wilderness."

Romance thrives in the great outdoors. Adam and Eve, Captain John Smith and Pocahontus, Tarzan and Jane, Charlie Allnutt and Rosie . . . many of our most famous couples did their famous coupling in the wilderness.

Aphrodisiacal as nature can be, there are pitfalls associated with sex in the Great Outdoors. One pitfall is that smooching hikers might fall in a pit. Another is the potential for frostbite to exposed portions of the human anatomy. Frost isn't the only thing that can bite tender regions—gnats, for example, can nibble rustic lovers in places they might be reluctant to scratch in public (unless they're professional baseball players, who'll scratch anything that itches even if they're on network television). As protection from gnats and their ilk, unwary sweethearts may be tempted to seek refuge in sleeping bags. This is always a mistake. There is a Universal Law which admits of no exception decreeing that the zipper of the sleeping bag always sticks whenever people try to make whoopee. Fiddling with a stuck zipper is ludicrous enough to induce giggling and frustrating enough to induce stress, either of which can have disastrous results. The answer is to keep a razor-sharp hunting knife handy to slash open the sleeping bag—ruining an item that set you back $500 is flamboyantly romantic. It also fills the tent with fluffy little feathers to tickle your fancy (to speak only of your fancy).

WHAT'S WHAT &
WHO'S WHO

Organizations

If you want to be a card-carrying wilderness-lover, or seem like one, there are all manner of clubs you can join, so many that both the National Wildlife Federation and the Ecology Center of Southern California publish directories of them.

Eco-Tours

The bluffer who has a yen for seriously wild places like Arctic tundra or Amazonian rain forest needs professional help to protect both self from the wilderness and wilderness from the self. Happily enough, dozens, perhaps hundreds, of outfits are in the business of eco-tourism, ecologically sensitive tourism that does no damage to wild places and may even convince their residents that there is more money to be made from tourism than from slash-and-burn agriculture. To consider just one example, the Massachusetts Audubon Society organizes expeditions to all manner of places — Madagascar, Iceland, Bali, Kenya — with real experts and sometimes an opportunity to help with turtle tagging or the like, at an average cost of about $2,500. The environmental journal *Buzzworm* indexes these eco-tourism ventures by kind and destination. Whether you want to scale cliffs, paddle a kayak, ride a camel, or photograph a whale, there's a firm eager to oblige. *Earthwatch* organizes paying volunteers to help scientific research in far-flung places for two- to three-week periods at costs from $650 to over $2,000 (average $1,300).

Wilderness Schools

If you want some expert advice in controlled situations, in which presumably there will be a rescuer when you find yourself dangling from a precipice, there are wilderness schools. One for beginners is the New-Age-slanted Reevis Mountain School of Self-Reliance.

If you know a thing or two about the outdoors or if you want to challenge yourself right away, try NOLS, the National Outdoor Leadership School. Founded by the colorful Paul Petzoldt in 1965, NOLS is a big operation. Even older is Outward Bound, with open-air campuses in five states. A four-day white-water course may cost $400, while a 90-day semester course may run over $3,000. If you're in New Jersey, consider the Tom Brown School of Tracking, Nature, and Wilderness Survival.

Mother Earth News, which ought to know, is high on BOSS, the Boulder Outdoor Survival School, saying, "While BOSS isn't the only competent wilderness survival school around, it's the oldest, it's the most challenging, and it teaches wilderness skills as they ought to be taught—in the wilderness."

Outdoor Magazines

If the thought of mosquitoes and frostbite and beaver fever create misgivings about actual camping, you might want to stay home and give the impression that you're at home in the wilderness by scattering outdoor magazines (and they are legion) around your parlor and bathroom. Many of the best are regional—there may be a magazine devoted to the very area you plan to pretend to have visited.

Some of the magazines you want may not be in the average library. If you're going to Canada, you might want to check *Borealis*, a magazine about Canadian parks and wilderness. There's often good stuff about outdoor skills in *Mother Earth News*, a magazine about rural lifestyles; libraries may avoid it from confusion with *Mother Jones*, the radical political journal. If you want a radical wilderness magazine, try *Earth First: The Radical Environmental Journal*.

For preschoolers, the National Wildlife Foundation publishes *Your Big Backyard*. For kids under eight, the Young Naturalist Foundation of Toronto publishes *Chickadee*. The *Your Big Backyard* kids graduate to *Ranger Rick;* the *Chickadee* kids graduate to *Owl*.

A glossy newcomer is the aforementioned *Buzzworm: The Environmental Journal*. In addition to the annual listing of eco-tours, it has suggestions for how to get involved in the struggle to protect the environment, splendid photographs, timely articles, and ads for expensive stuff that can help a bluffer pass for a mountaineer. (FYI: "buzzworm" is the Old-West nickname for rattlesnake.)

The Great Outdoors in Literature

When historians become experts on history, they don't have to visit history and clomp around in it getting all sweaty and bug-bitten—no, they learn about it from books. You can fob yourself off as the new Jim Bridger without venturing into anything swampier than your sauna by reading some of the classic literature about the Great Outdoors. Some bibliophiliacs actually schlepp heavy, hardbound books into the puckerbrush to read while camping, but it takes a hardy soul to read Goethe (or even Hardy) by flickering firelight with wood smoke in your eyes and mosquitoes in your ears. These books should be read while curled up in a comfy chair, next to a crackling fireplace, with snacks nearby, and falling snow beyond the front windows.

Ah, Wilderness!—(Eugene O'Neill, 1933) This play has nothing whatsoever to do with wilderness, but it's a lot less gloomy than O'Neill's more famous works.

Bambi—(Felix Salten, 1929) This exercise in instant folklore carries the pathetic fallacy about as far as it can go, with lots of rapture about the mystical beauty of the forest. Walt Disney's 1942 animated version inspired a Japanese sequel called *Bambi Meets Godzilla.*

The Compleat Angler—(Izaak Walton, 1653) This is not really a book about fishing. It's about . . . well, about this and that. It's the quaint, meditative book of an amiable old gent. Charles Lamb said, "It breathes the very spirit of innocence, purity, and simplicity of heart."

The End of Nature – (Bill McKibben, 1989) This ringing call for serious action to preserve the environment may make this book the *Silent Spring* of its generation.

The Lure of the Labrador Wild – (Dillon Wallace, 1905) In July of 1903, Wallace and companion Leonidas Hubbard paddled their canoe into the Susan River under the mistaken impression that it was the Nascaupee River. In the wilderness, one bay and the mouth of one river can look much like another, even to experts. Lost and trapped by winter, Wallace was found by trappers, but Hubbard died of starvation.

The Monkey Wrench Gang – (Edward Abbey, 1977) This comic adventure follows three men and a woman on a Luddite crusade through the Southwest, burning bulldozers and pulling up survey stakes. In an instance of life-copying-art, this book inspired the monkey wrenching of people like Dave Foreman of Earth First! The recently deceased Abbey is a guru for the radical environmentalists of the American West.

Silent Spring – (Rachel Carson, 1962) Few books change the world, but this one did, creating an awareness that pesticides were poisoning the natural world.

To Build a Fire – (Jack London, 1908) This is probably the best short story about woodsy lore (if one assumes that Hemingway's "Big Two-Hearted River" is really about something else entirely).

Travels in Arabia Deserta – (Charles Montagu Doughty, 1888) Doughty was one of those curious, intrepid Englishmen who went looking for his identity in wild places under the noonday sun. This classic was lavishly praised by T. E. Lawrence (a.k.a. Peter O'Toole), whose *Seven Pillars of Wisdom* (1926) is another monumental work in the same tradition.

A Week on the Concord and Merrimack Rivers — (Henry David Thoreau, 1849) HDT's paean to the wholesome outdoors is laced with digressions about literature and society and hifalutin stuff like that. His posthumously published *Maine Woods* (1864) includes accounts of his admiration for Indian guides Joe Aitteon and Joe Polis.

Woodswoman — (Anne LaBastille, 1978) An already-classic account of a woman alone in the woods by one of the nation's most influential ecologists.

Movies About the Great Outdoors

If reading a book from cover to cover strikes you as an unduly ardous undertaking, you may absorb your wilderness lore from the cinema.

Adventures of the Wilderness Family — (1975) A wholesome family abandons the urban rat race to go back to the land. If you like this one, it spawned two more or less identical sequels.

The African Queen — (1951) Unless you're willing to face more mosquitoes than Bogie and Kate faced, you should stay home.

Aguirre, the Wrath of God – (1972) If you think you might enjoy rafting, better check this one out first.

The Great Outdoors – (1988) This Dan Aykroyd/John Candy film is less amusing than a swarm of black flies in a honeymoon suite, but it boasts an apt title.

Jeremiah Johnson – (1972) Robert Redford plays a mountain man in the Old West. Redford is upstaged by splendid outdoor photography and by Will Geer. Redford's casting is apt because he's a genuine, real-life hero of the Great Outdoors, who works tirelessly on behalf of the environment.

Lord of the Flies – (1963) This movie proves beyond doubt that camping drives kids crazy.

Man's Favorite Sport – (1964) Howard Hawks directed this one with Rock Hudson as a writer of books about fishing who has never wet a line. Now *that's* bluffing!.

The Mosquito Coast – (1986) Harrison Ford plays the lead in this film version of the Paul Theroux novel about an American family homesteading in Central America. If you think your camping trip was a bummer, wait until you see this one.

Mountains of the Moon – (1990) Speke and Burton trek through Africa looking for the source of the Nile, even though they don't have any use for the thing if they find it.

The Naked Prey – (1966) Cornel Wilde is a Great White Hunter on safari who becomes the naked prey of an African tribe which gives him a head start into the jungle to be stalked by the tribe's best hunters.

This brutal survival story will give most bluffers all the jungle they want.

Never Cry Wolf – (1983) A Walt Disney film from the true story of Canadian Farlay Mowat, who ventured into the Arctic alone to study wolves. There are wonderful scenes as he goes so truly native that he runs naked with the animals and munches on mice lunches. A useful cautionary tale for the bluffer.

Names to Drop Around the Campfire and Elsewhere

Even when you're around the pub or the club, dropping these names will convince people you're steeped in wilderness lore.

Sir Robert Stephenson Smyth Baden-Powell

Lord Baden-Powell was the prototypical pukka sahib, stiff-upper-lip British colonial soldier (think of C. Aubrey Smith in *The Four Feathers*). He served in India and Afghanistan and fought the Zulu and Matabele in Africa. During the Boer War he held Mafeking with a small force for many months, winning promotion to major general. Back in England, he applied his methods for training soldiers to training boys, founding the Boy Scouts in 1908. King George V knighted him and asked Baden-Powell to devote himself entirely to this early recruiting effort. In 1910, he got his sister Agnes to organize Girl Guides along similar lines. The next time you see a Boy Scout helping an old lady across the street or starting a campfire by rubbing two

Girl Scouts together, remember it all started to preserve the Empire on which the sun was never to set.

Jim Bridger

Bridger (1804–81) was perhaps the most legendary Mountain Man of the American West. He led trapping expeditions through California, Idaho, Utah, and New Mexico. He was probably the first of European ancestry to see the Great Salt Lake. His tall tales of the Yellowstone region are now part of American folklore. Always eager to name things after himself, he founded Fort Bridger and opened Bridger's cut-off via Bridger's pass. He helped survey the route of the Union Pacific, and he measured the Bozeman Trail. Bridger was often mentioned in journals of the era with praise for his skill and intelligence. A bluffer is safe dropping Jim Bridger's name. There are debunkers about who will tell you Buffalo Bill Cody was largely invented by a charlatan who called himself Ned Buntline or that Jim Bowie is largely a creature of Hollywood fiction because his flamboyant knife is so photogenic, but to date, Jim Bridger has escaped the wrath of the revisionists.

Natty Bumppo

Natty Bumppo's name was so silly that James Fenimore Cooper gave him lots of nicknames: Leatherstocking, Hawkeye, Deerslayer, Pathfinder. Like the Lone Ranger, he had a faithful Indian companion, named Chingachgook (which Mark Twain says is pronounced "Chicago"). Bumppo's mastery of woodcraft was so subtle that he once followed the track of a cannonball through dense fog.

Cabeza de Vaca

Alvar Nuñez Cabeza de Vaca was the survivor par excellence. Second in command of an expedition from Spain to Florida in 1528, he made landfall near the mouth of the Mississippi. He turned up in Mexico City eight years later, having walked the whole way, enduring captivity and innumerable bad burritos.

Herman "Jackrabbit" Johannsen

Born in Norway in 1875, Johannsen was 40 when he showed up in Lake Placid and taught the Americans to climb mountains on skis. Johannsen was 72 when he placed third in the Stowe Derby, and at age 100 was still skiing. He lived to be 112.

John A. "Snowshoe" Johnson

An 1880s mailman who made regular 90-mile deliveries across the Sierras on homemade eleven-foot skis. They probably called him "Snowshoe" because "Eleven-foot Homemade Ski" Johnson sounds downright silly.

Bob Marshall

Called the "most efficient weapon of preservation in existence," Bob Marshall helped to save vast tracts of wilderness and to shape the very concept as we know it today. A map-eating hiker, his writings stirred a generation. The Bob Marshall Wilderness in Montana is named in his honor. If you like to wear sneakers on the trail, cite Bob Marshall as your authority. With virtually every expert touting sturdy leather hiking boots, Marshall liked sneaks because they're light, give a good grip, and dry quickly.

John Muir

Muir is the patron saint of American conservation. Born in Scotland in 1838, he grew up in Wisconsin and dreamed of exploring the Amazon until a bout of malaria sent him to California in 1868. He fell in love with the wilderness there, writing about it with the mixture of naturalist's detail and mystic's hyperbole that has characterized American nature freaks from the Transcendentalists like Thoreau to the New Agers like Peter Bigfoot of the Reevis Mountain School of Self-Reliance (where courses include "Inner Quest Self-Discovery Adventure," "Zen and the Art of Land Navigation," "Fasting Meditation Retreat," and "Practical Homeopathy"). Muir was responsible for the establishment of Yosemite National Park; he founded the Sierra Club in 1902 and took President Teddy Roosevelt on a camping trip. The 212-mile John Muir Trail along the high Sierra from Yosemite to the peak of Mt. Whitney is named in his honor.

Sacajawea

This Shoshone woman guided the Lewis and Clark expedition through the West in 1805 and 1806. Also known as Grass Maiden and Bird Woman, it was Sacajawea who made the expedition a success, leading them through difficult terrain she hadn't seen since girlhood. She lived to be 100, dying in Wyoming in 1884.

Henry David Thoreau

You can always find an apt quote from HDT. He said,

"I was determined to know beans," a remark easily made around most camp meals. His observations blend shrewd Yankee common sense with Transcendental blather: "As if you could kill time without injuring eternity," "Heaven is under our feet as well as over our heads," "Our horizon is never quite at our elbows." When you get the feel, you can bluff by making up your own, breezily announcing that "As Thoreau says, 'The proper sphere for humanity is the circle round the campfire'" or "As Thoreau says, 'The mysteries of the forest transcend the facts of the marketplace.'" If anyone calls your bluff, just say your ersatz quote comes from a letter from Thoreau to Louis Agassiz. If your bluff is still called, give up—few Americans have heard of Louis Agassiz, and anyone who claims to have read his correspondence is a better bluffer than you are.

FINAL EXAM

Before you venture into the wilderness, take this pop quiz to make certain you absorbed the essential information so painstakingly assembled for you in this handy compendium of camping lore.

1. If forced to start a fire without matches, you should
   (A) wait for lightning to strike.
   (B) rub two Boy Scouts together.
   (C) rub a Boy Scout and a Girl Scout together.
   (D) call in a napalm strike for your exact map coordinates.
   (E) use your monocle as a magnifying glass.

2. If lost in Canada, you must always
   (A) bear south.
   (B) vote Tory.
   (C) ice the puck.
   (D) follow the Northwest Passage.
   (E) wait for a Mountie.

3. Your latrine must be at least 150 feet from
   (A) your tent.
   (B) your water supply.
   (C) your breakfast.
   (D) all "Bear-Crossing" signs.
   (E) the nearest Howard Johnson's.

4. Famous, intrepid American explorers were
   (A) Harpo and Groucho.
   (B) Mario and Luigi.
   (C) Masters and Johnson.
   (D) Larry, Curly, and Moe.
   (E) Larry, Daryl, and Daryl.
   (F) Martin and Lewis.
   (G) Lewis and Clark.

5. If you're in a canoe on a strange river and you hear
   an ominous roaring noise in the mist ahead of you,
   you should
   (A) shoot the rapids.
   (B) shoot the falls.
   (C) shoot the works.
   (D) shoot the piano player.

GLOSSARY

This is the most useful part of the book for the daring bluffer who decides to pass as an expert on the Great Outdoors without venturing beyond anything wilder than drawing room or den. Lace your conversation with these terms to convince your friends that you could survive in the middle of the Amazon or Sahara with nothing but a Swiss Army knife and a pocketful of beef jerky.

Biome—Not a sports complex in the twin cities but an environmental community shaped by soil and climate.

Bivy Sack—A sack for a bivouac; intrepid mountaineers who feel a tent is too heavy will carry a bivy sack to zip into. As a bluffer, you don't want a bivy sack because you're apt to be uncomfortable enough in a tent. You don't want to go camping with anyone who plans to use a bivy sack—people like that are likely to make you wish you had decided to travel with the Donner Party instead.

Blaze—Nope, not a fire; a mark on a tree to show the trail. Old-timers slashed some bark from a tree to make a blaze, but today a dab of paint is used. Above the tree line, cairns (piles of rocks) may mark the trail.

Cant Dog—A sort of peavey.

Crampons – Crampons might be uncomfortable sanitary suppositories, but they're not; they're metal frames that attach to boots so their spikes give traction for climbing ice or hard snow.

Dingle Stick – A six- to eight-foot sapling to hang a pot above a fire. Also called a wangan stick, waumbec, gin pole, and chip-lok-wagan. By any name, the Micmac Indians believe it's bad luck to leave one standing over a dead fire.

Down – The opposite of up. Also the soft under-plumage of geese, prized as insulation – except when wet, or squashed. Alas for romance, synthetics such as PolarGuard or Hollofil II have certain advantages over down, being washable, nonallergenic, and superior when wet or crushed.

God's Country – No matter where you go in rural, rustic, or bucolic America, the locals will call the region "God's Country." This is as true in Texas as it is in Maine, as true in Oregon as in New Brunswick. By implication, where you come from in the city or the suburbs is *not* God's Country at all, but rather the realm of You-know-who. Whatever your theological opinions as to the Deity's geographic preferences, it's never prudent to engage the denizens of backwater outposts in debate on this subject. It's an article of faith among hayseeds and hermits that they dwell in "God's Country" and you don't. Anyone who disagrees can go back to Russia. Where they belong!

Gore-Tex – This sounds like a gruesome special effect from a Sam Peckinpah western: "When the shotgun blast hits the cowboy in the belly, get a tight closeup of the Gore-Tex!" In fact, it's a synthetic fabric, a laminate with the scientific moniker *polytetrafluoroethylene* (which explains why they call it Gore-Tex—anything is better than *polytetrafluoroethylene*). Gore-Tex is handy for tents and sleeping bags and windbreakers because it keeps rain out without keeping perspiration in. With nine billion holes per square inch, it's the most porous fabric around. Because every droplet of H_2O is surrounded by a negatively charged electron cloud, the billions of tiny droplets let water vapor out but repel raindrops because . . . Oh, forget it! The stuff costs a lot because it repels rain from outside while letting water vapor out.

Hogback—Some bluffers believe that hogback is what lumberjacks eat in Canada, but actually it's a sharp ridge with steep drops on both sides.

Krumholz—A Germany pastry. (Okay, we're kidding—krumholz is a batch of twisted, stunted trees fringing the tree line on a high mountain.)

Larrigans—High-top moccasins.

Lob Tree—In the old days, a portage was marked by a *lob tree*, a tall pine from which the upper branches had been chopped off.

Mal-de-Raquette—Aching hip joints and crotch caused by the bizarre straddle step required when snowshoeing.

Nessmuk—This sounds like a commercial brand of camp coffee but is actually the Indian name of George Washington Sears, old-time outdoorsman and author of the classic *Woodcraft*.

Peavey–A sort of cant dog.

Prayer Stick–Thin softwood stick whittled so that lots of curly shavings go every which way; a few of these will get a campfire going pronto.

Puckerbrush–A term of opprobrium common among Maine guides; for example, "You blankety-blank @#%* puckerbrush!" Actually, this term and some others are vague enough to vary with local usage. Dense thickets of short trees are puckerbrush, but the word is sometimes used as a synonym for scrub or krumholz or even cripplebrush.

Scree–Noise made by a camper who catches a bit of tender skin in a zipper by acting in undue haste during a midwinter emergency. Also loose rocks on a mountain slope; sometimes used to build scree walls to mark trails above a tree line where footsteps can do terrible damage to the fragile plant life of the alpine zone.

Scrub–What the loser at rock/scissors/paper has to do to the dishes. A dense thicket of short trees; in some regions applied only to hardwoods, to distinquish scrub from krumholz or puckerbrush, though not even Samuel Johnson and Noah Webster put together could define the differences among these terms to anyone's satisfaction.

Siwash–No, not a miracle detergent; a siwash camp is haphazard (such as finding yourself stranded in your canoe on a wild riverbank at nightfall) or just plain slovenly.

Snubbing–Not talking to your social inferiors? No! Snubbing is poling a canoe downstream.

Trapper Nelson – A professional wrestler? Nope. The wooden frame used to support huge loads; a.k.a. the Alaska packboard. The Trapper Nelson is still used, but only by incurable romantics, having been rendered obsolete by the tubular aluminum frame.

Whelan – This is not jazz slang, as in "The band was really whelan"; this is a lean-to tent, named after its designer, the famous Col. Townsend Whelan.

The biggest blun about the *Bluffer's Guides* is the title. These books are full of information — and fun.

NOW IN STOCK — $3.95

Bluff Your Way in Baseball
Bluff Your Way in British Theatre
Bluff Your Way in Computers
Bluff Your Way in the Deep South
Bluff Your Way in Football
Bluff Your Way in Golf
Bluff Your Way in Gourmet Cooking
Bluff Your Way in Hollywood
Bluff Your Way in Japan

Bluff Your Way in Management
Bluff Your Way in Marketing
Bluff Your Way in Music
Bluff Your Way in New York
Bluff Your Way in the Occult
Bluff Your Way in Paris
Bluff Your Way in Public Speaking
Bluff Your Way in Wine
Bluffer's Guide to Bluffing

NEW TITLES

Bluff Your Way in the Great Outdoors
Bluff Your Way in Home Maintenance
Bluff Your Way in Math
Bluff Your Way in Office Politics
Bluff Your Way in Philosophy
Bluff Your Way in Psychology
Bluff Your Way in Sex

To order any of the Bluffer's Guides titles above,
use the order form on the next page.

AVAILABLE SOON

Bluff Your Way in Basketball
Bluff Your Way in Dining Out
Bluff Your Way in Etiquette
Bluff Your Way in Fitness
Bluff Your Way in Las Vegas
Bluff Your Way in London
Bluff Your Way in Marriage
Bluff Your Way in Parenting
Bluff Your Way in Politics
Bluff Your Way in Relationships